P9-AZV-387

Peace Mandala
Coloring Book
from children around the world

By Monique Mandali, Editor

By the same author:
Everyone's Mandala Coloring Book (Volume 1)
Everyone's Mandala Coloring Book (Volume 2)
Everyone's Mandala Coloring Book (Volume 3)

Copyright © 2000 by Monique Mandali

First printing, August 2000
Second printing, January 2001
Third printing, January 2004
Fourth printing, March 2008

All rights reserved, including the right to reproduce this book or
parts thereof, in any form, except for the inclusion of brief quotations in a review.

ISBN 978-1-58592-061-7
Printed in Canada

Published by Mandali Publishing,
P.O. Box 219, Helena, Montana 59624
(1-800-347-1223), in cooperation with SkyHouse Publishers,
an imprint of The Globe Pequot Press.

Design, typesetting, and other prepress work by
SkyHouse Publishers

Distributed by The Globe Pequot Press,
P.O. Box 480, Guilford, CT 06437-0480
or call 1-800-243-0495

also distributed by
New Leaf, Devorss,
Koen, Baker & Taylor, Partners, and Ingram.

Visit our website and online catalog: www.mandali.com

Preface

I knew that my fourth mandala coloring book would be special. Aware of a long-ago dream in which I saw myself leading children of different races, ethnic backgrounds and languages to a peninsula where East and West peacefully meet, a friend suggested I involve children. And so the idea was born to ask girls and boys around the world to design Peace Mandalas to help spread seeds of harmony among humankind at the turn of a new millennium.

The call went out in the fall of 1998 via my website and thousands of flyers. I held my breath, not knowing if anyone would respond. Months later, as if by magic and no doubt with the encouragement of parents, teachers and spiritual leaders, Peace Mandalas started to arrive. I wish I could have included all of them; sadly, that was not possible. I selected some of the best and then asked the artists to tell me about themselves.

My "Peace Mandala children" are truly citizens of the world and quite remarkable. Several have traveled to or lived in different countries, consider themselves bicultural and are bilingual. Jessica, her brother Derek, and Emmeline are fluent in Chinese and English. The Nepalese girls speak Nepali and English; Max knows French and English. A member of the Northern Cheyenne Indian Tribe, Bernice effortlessly switches between her native tongue and English. Marieke and my daughter Ingrid feel equally at home in cultures on either side of the North Atlantic Ocean.

These girls and boys emerged from diverse corners on earth. Fedde and Rafaëlle reside near bustling European world ports, Rotterdam and Antwerp. By contrast, Marieke lives in a semi-arid Montana village with fewer than 250 inhabitants, dogs and cats included. At the other end of the American continent Paula makes her home in the cosmopolitan capital of Argentina, Buenos Aires. Thousands of miles away in Central Asia, Tshering and my Nepalese daughter Jyotsna live in the foothills of the majestic, snow-capped Himalayas. Kenna's world in Brisbane, Australia, is filled with tropical plants and the Pacific Ocean.

Not surprisingly, all the children like to draw; many paint and play musical instruments. Helen and Fedde love acting; Jessica and Emmeline sing and dance. Several children participate in baseball, volleyball, basketball, track, swimming and soccer. Bernice likes riding horses; brothers Matias and Piero share a passion for paragliding. Kenna simply loves to make people laugh.

As to what they'd like to do when they grow up, Helen wants to be a famous artist or clothing designer. Bernice and Tshering intend to be doctors, Paula a doctor or psychologist. Alison wants to visit the Galapagos Islands and be an author. Sanjiv, Piero and Derek aspire to be professional soccer players, Max a baseball player. But then again, Sanjiv may become a computer engineer and Piero a paraglider. Rafaëlle would love to train dolphins. Jessica wants to be a musician; Allison, a singer or artist. Being a chef, owning a chocolate shop and working for justice are Kenna's dreams while Matias is tugged between commercial and electronic engineering. Jackie, Fedde and Marieke want to work with animals, alive or very dead, and be a veterinarian, zoologist or paleontologist. At 6 and the youngest of my Peace Mandala children, Chris wants to do "everything." Well, he has a lot of time to decide.

The children's Peace Mandalas, in their original form all drawn freehand, express peace in different ways. Perhaps the most thought-out is Tshering's first design. With passion and clarity she explains: "In the center are symbols of three world religions: Buddhism, Christianity and Hinduism. The symbol OM, the first and most sacred sound in the universe, in Hinduism (lower center) and Buddhism (upper right) means peace to me. The doves are also symbols of peace and children of the world unite to preserve it. The earth, trees, river and mountains are resources that we must preserve." Her second mandala is filled with peace symbols found in Buddhist temples and monasteries.

For Helen and Bernice, feeling at peace is being in nature; for Sarah, it is imagining herself surrounded with sunshine, flowers and butterflies. Other mandalas are more abstract. Jyotsna's design makes her feel "very happy," Piero's "filled with joy." Kenna's means "that all people are united and everyone is special." For Paula* and Matias, peace and harmony reside in the center. Emmeline's design "has the feeling of warmth and coolness, of happiness when you are lonely, of peace on every land and in every heart."

When asked about their wishes for the future, all children echo "no more wars, no more racism, no more prejudice." Emmeline hopes "that people will live in peace regardless of their skin, hair or eye color." Piero wants "tranquility and love for the family." Fedde, whose design graces the cover of this book, hopes that "Peace Mandalas will help people around the world have happiness and find peace."

The last Peace Mandala was drawn by Kristy Pokorny, a 54-year-young artist and teacher. It emerged while meditating on the word "peace" and "prayer for the family." Kristy's design embraces so perfectly the children's thoughts and feelings that I decided to include it. Besides, as precocious and mature as my Peace Mandala children may be, they are still children, so it is natural that they be given a Mandala Mother, an honor Kristy gracefully accepts.

---

* The religious symbols in Paula's Peace Mandala represent, starting from the top, clockwise: Chinese religions, Japanese religions, Buddhism, Christianity, Islam, Hinduism, Native religions, Judaism.

The magic of mandalas

Mandalas have been used through the ages to meditate, promote healing and soothe body, mind and spirit. Regardless of their cultural backgrounds, children intuitively know that designing or coloring mandalas generates peace and harmony. As these feelings ripple like waves of energy from our quiet center, they touch those around us. No one knows how many mandalas it will take before humankind experiences more tranquility. Perhaps a billion. The exact number is not important. What does matter is knowing that every time we color a mandala, and especially a Peace Mandala designed by a child, we nurture and strengthen our collective vision for a more peaceful world.

To all the girls and boys who helped me create this special book, thank you. You give us hope.

Monique Mandali

NOTE TO CHILDREN OF THE WORLD: you may continue to send your original Peace Mandala designs to MANDALI PUBLISHING for possible selection in future volumes. Make sure to include your name, address and birth date.

Monique Mandali, M.A., is a transpersonal psychotherapist in Montana and author of several popular mandala coloring books. She offers mandala workshops for teachers, health care professionals, therapists, and the public at large. Contact Monique at 800-347-1223 or via e-mail: monique@mandali.com.

Tshering. 15
Kathmandu. Nepal

Jackie. 12
Montana. USA

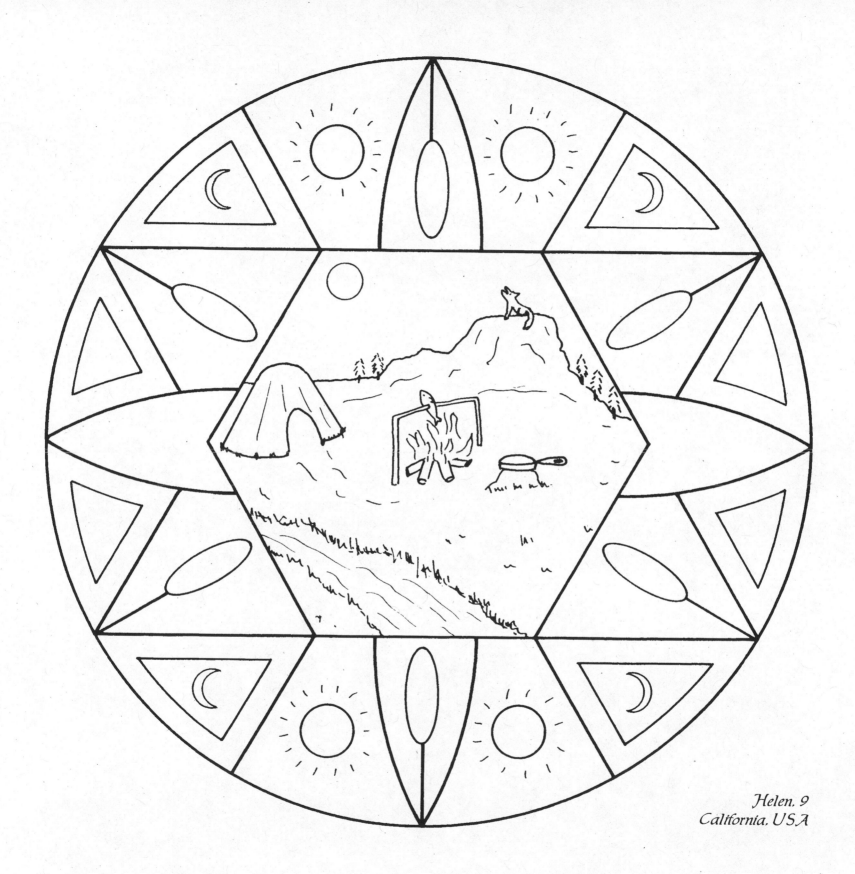

Helen. 9
California, USA

Kenna. 12
Brisbane. Australia

Ingrid. 11
Oregon. USA/Belgium

Jyotsna. 13
Talamarang. Nepal

Sanjiv. 11
Illinois. USA/Sri Lanka

Allison. 9
Rhode Island, USA

Matías. 12
Rancagua. Chile

Bernice. 11
Montana. USA

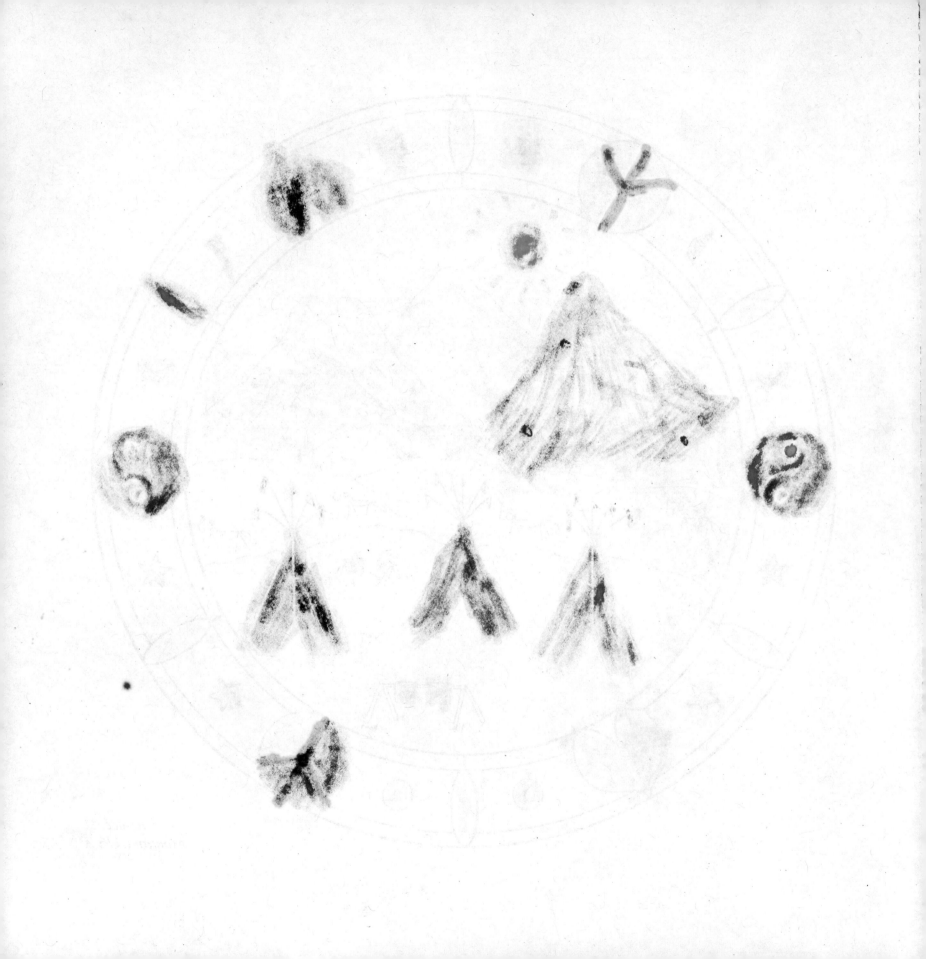

Alison. 12
California. USA

Paula. 14
Buenos Aires. Argentina

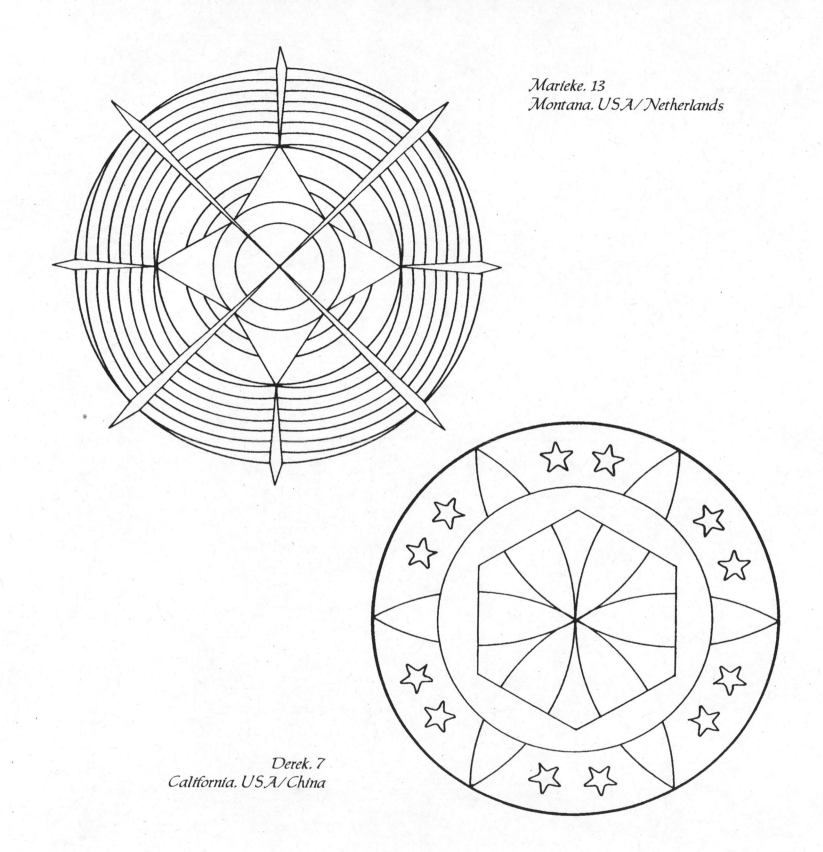

Marieke. 13
Montana. USA/Netherlands

Derek. 7
California. USA/China

Chris. 6
California. USA

Rafaëlle. 7
Antwerp. Belgium.

Emmeline, 10
North Carolina, USA/China

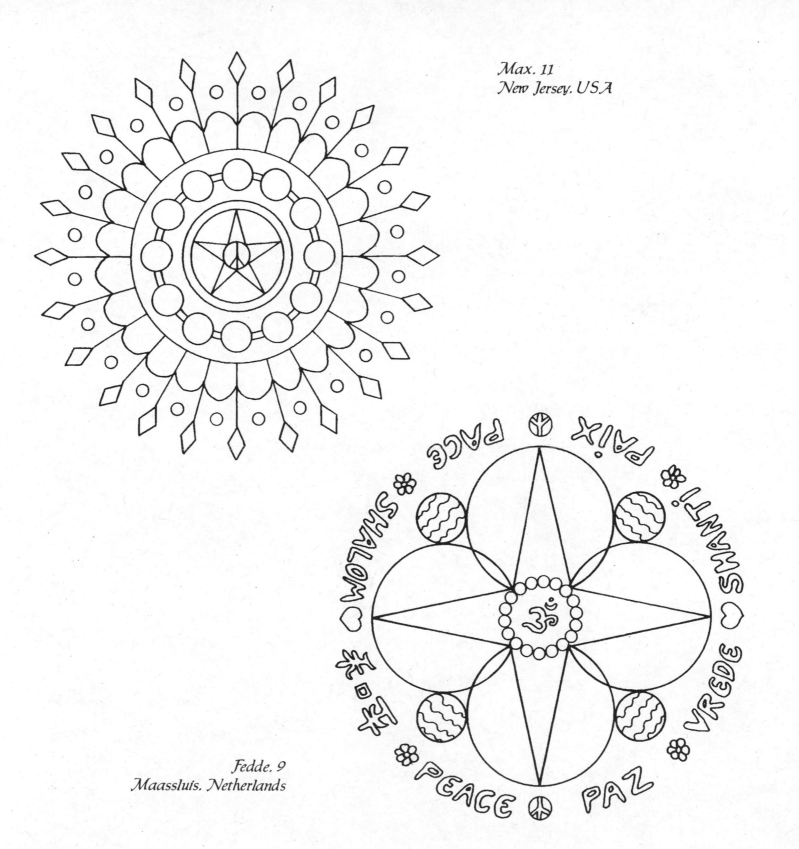

Max. 11
New Jersey. USA

Fedde. 9
Maassluis. Netherlands

Piero, 8
Rancagua, Chile

Kristy Pokorny, 54
Illinois, USA